Inspiration from Olympic Athletes for Students

ISBN: 978-1-61206-238-9

To order this book at quantity discounts, contact AlohaPublishing@gmail.com

Printed in the United States

To all the Olympic athletes who inspire the us to go beyond mediocrity.

Contents

"Motivation is what gets you started. Habit is what keeps you going."

Jim Ryun
USA Track and Field
Olympic Silver Medalist 1968

He was the first high schooler to run under four minutes for the mile.

"The formula for success is simple: practice and concentration then more practice and more concentration."

Babe Didrikson Zaharias
USA Track and Field
Olympic Gold Medalist 1932

She is widely regarded as one of the greatest female athletes of all time.

"We all have dreams. But in order to make dreams come into reality, it takes an awful lot of determination, dedication, self-discipline and effort."

Jesse Owens
USA Track and Field
Four-time Olympic Gold Medalist

In 1935, he set three world records and tied another, all in under an hour, in what has been called "the greatest 45 minutes ever in sport".

"People make a big mistake when they say, 'I need to be motivated.' You motivate yourself. I might inspire somebody, but that person has to be motivated within themselves first.

Billy Mills
USA Track and Field
Olympic Gold Medalist 1964

His 1964 victory is considered one of the greatest Olympic upsets because he was a virtual unknown going into the event.

"It is better to look ahead and prepare than to look back and regret."

Jackie Joyner Kersee
USA Track and Field
Four-time Olympic Medalist ('84, '88, '92, '96)
She has been called the world's greatest woman athlete.

"Growing up in the time of Title IX – it was passed when I was 10 – I got a front-row seat to so many great moments in women's sports. Of course, I didn't know it at the time."

Janis Klecker
USA Marathon Team
Won the 1992 US Olympic Trials Marathon in Houston
She was an American record holder in the 50K in 1983.
Mom of six, her son, Joe Klecker, made the 2021 Olympic team for Track and Field.

"I think women make good runners because they're so good at multitasking, and it's something they can fit into their busy schedules. Running is more accessible and affordable than a lot of other sports and fitness activities. It can also be very social, which draws women in."

Joan Benoit Samuelson
USA Marathon Team
Olympic Gold Medalist 1984
She is widely considered the greatest female long-distance runner in American history.

The only limitations are those you place on yourself and those you allow other people to place on you.

Jean Driscoll
USA Olympic and Paralympic team
Two Time Olympic Silver Medalist
She participated in four Summer Paralympic Games
She won a total of five gold, three silver, and four bronze medals in events ranging from 200 meters to the marathon.

"I think when you have a disability people are always putting limitations on you, telling you, even in a nice way, what you can't do. My attitude to that has always been: You can't tell me that. I'll show you."

Louise Savage
Australia Olympic and Paralympic team
A four-time Paralympian of the Year ('94, '96, '97, '98)
She joined the ranks of the Paralympic Hall of Fame as one of the world's most outstanding athletes and Australia's most successful Paralympian.

"Even when I'm old and can't move anymore, I'll still be able to go to a game and watch the families exude pride over their little girls and know that I had something to do with it."

Teresa Edwards
USA Women's Basketball
Four-time Olympic Gold Medalist ('84, '88, '96, '00)
She is the only female basketball player to win five Olympic medals (four of them gold).

"No matter how far life pushes you down, no matter how much you hurt, you can always bounce back."

Sheryl Swoopes
USA Women's Basketball
Three-time Olympic Gold Medalist ('96, '00, '04)
She was inducted in the Naismith Memorial Basketball Hall of Fame in 2016.

"If I am only remembered for being a basketball player, I believe I will have failed in my job on this planet."

Ruthie Bolton
USA Women's Basketball
Two-time Olympic Gold Medalist

"I am a big believer in visualization. I run through my races mentally so that I feel even more prepared."

Allyson Felix
USA Track and Field
Four-time Olympian ('04, '08, '12, '16); Nine-time Olympic Medalist (6 golds, 3 silvers)
She is one of the most decorated female Olympians in track and field history.

"Age is just a number."

Dara Torres
USA Swimming
12-time Olympic Medalist
Former world record holder in three events.
She currently holds the record for oldest swimmer to earn a place on the US Olympic team, and she is the first and only swimmer to represent the US in five Olympic Games.

"I believe it's our responsibility to show our communities the value of all people, to celebrate difference, and to take a stand for acceptance and inclusion."

Julie Foudy
USA Soccer
She is a two-time FIFA Women's World Cup champion and two-time Olympic Gold Medalist
She was the first American and first woman to win the FIFA Fair Play Award for her work against child labor.

"Failure happens all the time. It happens every day in practice. What makes you better is how you react to it."

Mia Hamm
USA Soccer
She is a two-time FIFA Women's World Cup champion and two-time Olympic Gold Medalist
At 15 years old, she became the youngest player on the US Women's National Soccer Team.

"I have a passion for life that allows me to make the most of my days and fill them with work and play."

Nick Symonds
USA Track and Field
He is a six-time US National 800 meters champion. He has competed in the 800m at two Olympic Games, reaching the semi-finals in Beijing in 2008.

"The best thing to do when you find yourself in a hurting or vulnerable place is to surround yourself with the strongest, finest, most positive people you know."

Kristin Armstrong
USA Cycling
Three-time Olympic Gold Medalist
Winner of the women's individual time trials ('08, '12, '16).
She is the only cyclist in Olympic history to win three gold medals in the same discipline and the oldest female cycling medalist of all time.

"When I run, I feel God's pleasure."

Eric Liddell
Scotland Olympic Team
Olympic Gold Medalist 1924
He is also known as 'The Flying Scotsman.'

"It's really kind of overwhelming. It's humbling. I've looked at what's happened in my life and now I can see how I helped shift the ability for women of color to run long distances."

Marilyn Manning Mimms
USA Track and Field
Olympic Gold Medalist 1968.
She was the first black woman to ever win the 800 meters Olympic event

"Men of success meet with tragedy. It was the will of God that I won the Olympics, and it was the will of God that I met with my accident. I accepted those victories as I accept this tragedy. I have to accept both circumstances as facts of life and live happily."

Abebe Bikila
Ethiopia Marathon team
Olympic Gold Medalist 1960
He was the first black African Olympic gold medalist.

"Life is often compared to a marathon, but I think it is more like being a sprinter; long stretches of hard work punctuated by brief moments in which we are given the opportunity to perform at our best."

Michael Johnson
USA Track and Field
Four-time Olympic Gold Medalist and eight-time World Championship Gold Medalist
He is generally considered one of the greatest and most consistent sprinters in the history of track and field.

"Don't put a limit on anything. The more you dream, the further you get."

Michael Phelps
USA Swimming
23-time Olympic Gold Medalist
He holds the all-time record for most Olympic gold medals.

"My message is to never quit, never give up. When you have a little trouble here and there, just keep fighting. In the end, it will pay off."

Gabby Douglas
USA Gymnastics
Olympic All-Around Champion 2012
She was the first African American to become the Olympic individual all-around champion

"You have to remember that the hard days are what make you stronger. The bad days make you realize what a good day is."

Aly Raisman
USA Gymnastics
Two-time Olympian ('12, '16)
She is the second-most decorated Olympic gymnast in American history behind Shannon Miller with six Olympic medals.

"You have to let fear go. Another lesson is you just have to believe in yourself; you just have to. There's no way around it. No matter how things are stacked against you, you just have to every time."

Venus Williams
USA Tennis
Five-time Olympic Medalist
She is the most decorated Olympic tennis player in American history.

"Passion is a huge prerequisite to winning. It makes you willing to jump through hoops, go through all the ups and downs and everything in between to reach your goal."

Kerri Walsh Jennings
USA Beach Volleyball
Three-time Olympic Gold Medalist
She is the beach volleyball career leader in career victories and career winnings

"Never underestimate the power of dreams and the influence of the human spirit. We are all the same in this notion: The potential for greatness lives within each of us."

Wilma Rudolph
USA Track and Field
Three-time Olympic Gold Medalist
Her Olympic successes in the 60s helped elevate women's track and field in the United States.

"The ones who are successful are the ones who really want it. You have to have that inner drive otherwise it's not going to work out."

Kerri Strug
USA Gymnastics
Olympic Gold Medalist 1996
She was part of the women's gymnastics team known as the "Magnificent Seven" who represented the U.S. and won the 1996 Olympics.

I'd made it this far and refused to give up because all my life I had always finished the race.

Louis Zamperini
USA Track and Field
He competed in the 5000m at the 1936 Berlin Olympics. He was the subject of the popular book and movies, *Unbroken* and the *sequel Unbroken: Path to Redemption*

Acknowledgments

Many thanks to Beth Berger for research on this book. My extreme gratitude to Heather Goetter for cover and interior design direction. Thanks to the Olympic and Paralympic athletes who have been my friends over the years. It's true, I started following the stories of Olympic champions when I was young. The words they said were powerful enough to keep me dreaming about new goals long after my years as a competitive athlete were over.

About the Author

Maryanna Young had an interest in Olympic Sports since the age of seven. She was fascinated by what characteristics made ordinary individuals into champions. In college she was a Division I student athlete in Cross Country and Track & Field. She competed as a member of the USA Korfball Team at the World Cup in Eindhoven, Belgium. The majority of her professional career she served as a sports agent and business development specialist for Olympic athletes.

Other books by this author

How to Write a Nonfiction Book in 12 Hours

25 Absolutely Essential Things You Need to Know about Writing and Publishing a Book

Million Dollar Days: What if You Were Given a Million Dollars for Just One Day?

Made in the USA
Las Vegas, NV
17 September 2025

28107353R00046